A pu

A collection of punny pieces by AFGL
with illustrations by Nipper

Published by Alan F G Lewis

First published 1977 by Alan F G Lewis, 27 Odds Farm Estate, Wooburn Common, High Wycombe, Bucks, HP10 0LA

ISBN 0 9505547 0 7

Printed by C. Nicholls & Company Ltd
The Philips Park Press, Manchester

FOREWORD
Prow

FORWORD
Yes

FOURWORD
Quartet

FORWARD

I told her no sensible man
Would take her dancing
In her bikini
So she went
With a little moron

My singing teacher says I need a tonic
My snooker friends advise a break
The drug pusher suggested I take a trip
My tailor says I could do with a change
The bookseller recommends I turn over a new leaf
The pharmacist insists I take five
My osteopath maintains I need a wrest
The lost-property office says I should turn it in
So I'm taking a holiday
To escape the constant advice

As the judge was in chambers
He was incommoded by my request
And I have to see him
At his convenience.
It's a potty system

The service to
Bury
Is presumably
Inter
City

Last knight
A bishop
Was rooked
By a queen
Selling pawn
In the King's Road

INFLATION IN THE CITY

The doorman
Is in a jamb.
The bunny girl
Is feeling the pinch.
The fan dancer
Is in a ticklish situation.
The barman
Is in a tight corner.
The professional escort
Is being driven to extremities.
And the drug pusher
Is in a fix.

Just had a wartime dream
I was with a squad
Of eighty yes girls

Back-seat driving
Is a form of duel control

I could tell from his
Pot plants
That he was a trug addict

Goblin your food
Is bad for your elf

She'll do anything
For a song or a drink.
So we offered a roundelay

Bambi could never have been
A mother
If her hart hadn't been
In the right place

Though I lost my temper
And yelled at everyone
In the motorists' shop
I couldn't get a solenoid

A capital lover
Writes small letters
But believes in largesse for
Sex

I'LL BE WITH YOU
in two sex, said the hermaphrodite
in half a tick, said the vivisectionist
in two shakes, said the freemason
in half a mho, said the electrician
in a trice, said the Third Man
in necks to no time, said the executioner
in a flash, said the magician
in an instant, said the marketing man
in a twinkling, eye said

When a liar gets pharyngitis
He loses his vice

When Eve offered Adam
The apple
They realised for the first time
They had no cloves

Spring is here.
Saprise! Saprise!

The pound
Was sound
Till we went decibel

Those who work for peanuts
Are always shelling out
And it's those with cashew
Can salt some away

Erminaduke and Marmtrude
Are pen-friends.
They've been exchanging letters
For some time

A white lie
Is aversion
Of the truth

ON BEING FORTY
Is life really
Four nought
Or is it time
Two score
And XL?

She said I was
The kind she could go for.
Wish I'd been
The kind she could stay for

If they asked me what
Shakespeare called the Globe
I'd politely say
A wooden O

When everything is in triplicate
You can't see the wood
For the coppice

I told the solitary pedestrian
He had BO
And he replied
'That's why I wore cologne'

His paper business
Folded
His brassiere business
Went bust
His direct mail concern
Was written off
His submarine company
Went under
And his posters
Went to the wall

I put all my savings
On a horse
And now I'm a saddler
But wiser man

To refuse a cigarette
Just say
No tar

He's a fair boxer.
His swing
Can make a round a bout

A maxi skirt
Is fine in a bungalow
But a mini
Is better for stares

He's doing much butter
Since he found a whey
Of milking his firm of expenses
When none have been in curd

Is a group of trainee
Secret service agents
Aspiring?

I've just seen a stage version
Of the Female Eunuch.
The cast rating was excellent

Most pop fans
Are star-craving mad

LOVE LETTER
You have the kind of XXX
That I cipher

He's a bit of a quiet fish
I'm told he's a piano tuna

When the witch said
Abradacabra
Nothing happened.
She's a hopeless speller

VALENTINE RHYME

My heart and I
Call to you
But you're too deaf
To Eros

I asked them for a quotation
For a new wall safe
And they said
St Matthew vi. 19

Because she has
A 39.37 inch bust
Men love to metre
But I don't know what they see
In the two decimal places

My children prefer punishment
In the heat of the moment
Rather than waiting
Till I scold

A lady cellist
Just lost her job
Through making her scherzo short

Baldness
Is a kind of failure.
Wish I'd made the greyed

The Apathy Society
That I founded is doing well:
Last year our membership
Fell by half

Her millinery is old hat
Her carriages are hackneyed
Her picture frames are passé
Her walnut loaf is dated
And her broomhandle is stale

The reproof of the pudding
Is in the repeating

A gentleman is someone
Who always offers a lady
Deceit

At night I lie awake
Wondering what I'd do
If ever I suffered from
Insomnia

Having brought the house down
He said he didn't know
It was liable to claps
(Which seemed applausible storey)

INFLATUATION
My heart used to pound
When I saw her
But now it only does
A bob or two

SLIMMING MOTTO
Here today
And gaunt tomorrow

When he applied for the job
Of human cannon-ball
They took him like a shot

Writing these is easy.
You jest
Put pun
To paper

The fish-processing factory
Had a vacancy
But I couldn't fillet

There are two kinds of people:
Married and cynical

When I'm stoned
I get a little boulder

When she said
I could make her mine
I knew
She was a gold-digger

SONG FOR SMALL MINORITIES

They expect us to flea
But weevil not be moved
Because their propaganda is all lice
And mite is right

If British Rail introduce
More no-smoking compartments
Will it reduce
Pullmanary complaints?

A terrorist believes
He has a right
To live and bereave

The old Christmas spirit
Is like artificial holly:
Dead and berried

When he's plastered
He's a bundle of laths

An operatic reputation
Has to be earned.
It's no one's Bayreuth

If a man asks a woman
To help him with a crowbar
It's because
He can't lever alone

He's highly strung
And describes himself
As self-taut.
(I think the spelling
Is intensional)

Holiday affairs
Are volcanic
And it's tuff
When your lava cools off

He found his wife had a lover
When he caught the fast twain

I was neutral
Till a live wire
Promised me the earth

Though he worked hard
Teaching me the art of rowing
He never got it into my scull

If bar drinks go metric
I hope it's
Schooner rather than litre

I'm a bit chicken
Where birds are concerned
But I somehow need less pluck
If she's well dressed

Courtship
Is when you try each other
For sighs

I invented a boy jelly-baby
But it didn't sell well
Because the novelty
Soon wore off

She would keep
Harping on about tidiness
Blowing her own trumpet
And drumming it into me
That I mustn't fiddle
With my hair.
I think she was instrumental
In our divorce.

The hotel porter refused
To carry my baggage
So I punched him.
My case comes up next week

Soupçon
Is French for a small amount
Only morceau

He swept her off her feet
But she realised it was just flannel
When he tried to sponge on her
For the price of a wring
So she gave him the brush off
And made a clean break

A tied pub
Is presumably
A trussed house

To win the status race
You need two loos

Crosswords are infuriating.
They're always putting 1 across
Which tends to get 1 down

When she said 'Howdah do
Take a pew
You look divan'
I thought 'This is sit'
But I was throne aside
When she decided to settle
For a pouffe
A sort of plinth charming
Who promised to support her
For the rest of her dais.
Next time I'll be more chairy

Chalet or shanty?
It's a decision he should
Dwell on

It isn't the confetti
That gives newlyweds away
But the rice to the bedroom

He claims the footprint
Is of the Abominable Snowman
Yeti's evidence is spoorious

Smoking
Is the hot tip
That's a dead cert

He called me a pessimist.
I don't know what it means
But I bet it's something
Horrible

I do envy artists.
I'd give my right ear
To be able to paint
Like Van Gogh

An Alpine hydroelectric scheme
Presumably produces
Off-peak electricity

Blood is thicker than water
And kith is sweeter than wine

He rants like an old sea-dog
But his barque
Is worse than his bight

Is humble pie
Appease pudding?

His suit

Prow

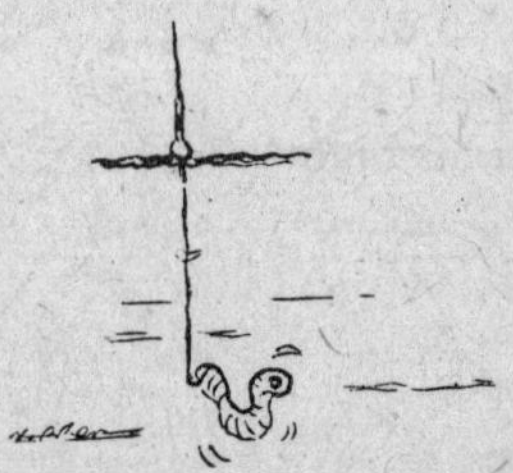

Bait

Hirsute

Prowess

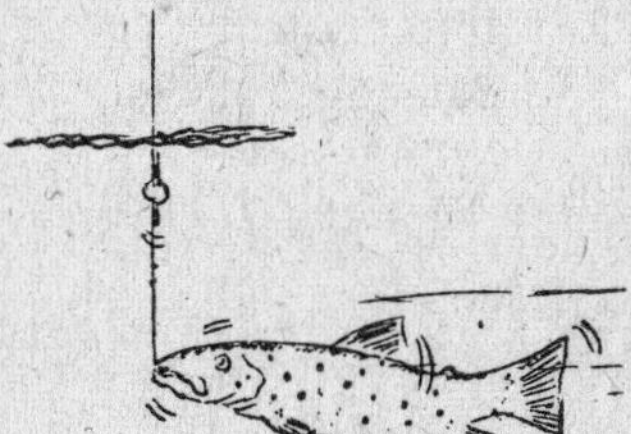

Rebate

When she invited him
Into her tent
She hoped the guy
Would stay

My tax form has two headings:
INCOME OWED US
And
INCOMMODE YOU

My new sex manual
Is all embracing

THE INVENTOR
of engraving made a pretty penny
of cardboard made a packet
of astrology made a fortune
of rooms made a tidy bit
of carpets made a pile
of annular sweets made a mint
of photocopying made a million

SEVEN AGES OF MAN
Oat age
Rote age
Vote age
Gloat age
Bloat age
Goat age
Dotage

She's the May Queen
I hope to May King

His pictures
Are atmospheric.
He paints by nimbus

She loves swarthy men
And never lets a dago by

I was going to pieces
Till the doctor told me
Not to exerpt myself

He's a theatre buff
With a tendency to fawn

Monogamy
Leaves a lot
To be desired

If his new secretary
Isn't sweet in the daytime
And a little tart at night
He'll saccharin the morning

EASTER DIET
Ovoid chocolate

If there are plenty more
Pebbles on the beach
Why haven't I had
A shingle offer?

I've had this cough
For exactly seven days.
My doctor says
It's just a wee cold

ADVICE TO THIEVES
Wear a stocking mask.
Denier won't be recognized

She put her arms around me,
Squeezed and said
"This is my only vice"

When she dropped a line
me

my spirits
To raise

s inclined to think
a
I w

h
S might not be on the level
e

So I w
e
n
t straight down to see her
.

I THINK THAT I SHALL NEVER

Yew witch Hazel
It's plane
I'm sycamore poplar girls
And aspen alder time
On the beech
And pine to cedar day
When I'm maple to say
"Hazel lime yours,
Cumquat may"

He has 150 cattle.
He thought there were 147
Till he rounded them up

I could tell
From her 41-31-37 measurements
That she was in her primes

The Three Wise Men
Each carried only one gift
Because they had believed
In travelling light

I've been going
Backwards and forwards
To the doctor for treatment
And am half cured.
Now I only go forwards

SEASONAL TOPICS
Spring board
Summer salt
Autumn attics
Winter green

She's clearly a verse to him
So how he stanza
I don't know.
Perhaps it's her lovely L-E-G's

Schnapps
And hock
Are my favourite
Teutonics

A true adman
Writes the prose
And cons

Don't put too many adaptors
Into one socket.
They confuse

SEX LIFE

Nineteen plenty
Twenty-nine flirty
Thirty-nine forte
Forty-nine thrifty
Fifty-nine three score
Sixty-nine eventually

She told me he was just
A travelling companion
But I sensed
Arrival

"George Bernard Shore was born in Island"
Is both a littoral mistake
And a printer's Eire

Please excuse
Ym shguoc dna sezeens
But I've got this
Terrible code

I've put my money
Into a new girlie magazine
So I can take
Accrued interest

Women who wear
Fishnet tights
Are usually happy
To shoal their legs

RE-COLLECTIONS
A pride of plaice
A flock of mattresses
A herd of old jokes
A clutch of straws
A fleet of foot
A litter of picnickers
A haul of fame
A peal of strippers
A cast of fishermen
A crew of interest
A brood of tea
A s'warm of summer greetings
A s'cool of winter greeetings

Some tie marriage knots
With gold
While others prefer
Platinum

She often gave me a buzz
At the office during the day
But I found out she was
A fly by night

A pub is the only place
Where you say cheers
When they greet you with boos

Each night our furry
Purry cat
Would onomatopoeia

Weight-lifting
Is a hard way
To hernia living

With a glass of whine
You can have a wail of a time
Till the bawl is over

I was young
Once.
Wish it had been
Twice.

MATERIAL WITNESS
She was often canvassed
But never suede

To cope now and then
With the ins and outs
Of the comings and goings
And ups and downs
He's found a new approach
That's quite a departure

Why piccolo profession
Like music
That's full of viol practices
Confirmed lyres
Old fiddles
And bass desires?
For the lute, of course

We live on a triangular estate.
I think we've got the right angle
But you should see
Some of the squares
On the other two sides

The Moses film project
Was abandoned
After they'd seen the rushes

The king dissolved Parliament
And then took the solute

Conscience
Is ought-to suggestion

When the
psychiatrist
asked me to
outline my
obsessions
I told him
I had none
so I can't
see why he
went on
about
snakes

She has a flare
For the piano.
You can see by her
Very light touch

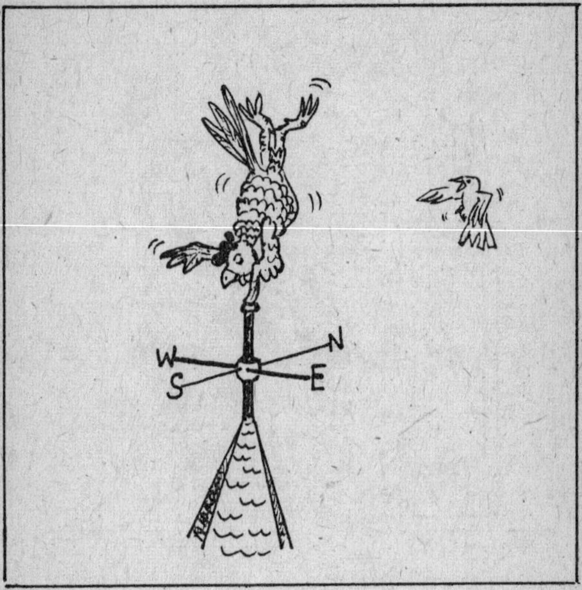

Weather vane or not
He's certainly cocky

The rigging can be
String
But mast bands should be
Brass

Don Juan
Carved nicks in the bedpost
So he could count
The noches

He put his flannel shirt
On a horse
Because it was napped

He called me woodenhead
So I gave him
A piece of my mind.
Now he's got
A chip on his shoulder

When she said
I could kiss her on the groyne
I knew I was on
A shore thing

Once upon a time I used
To mispell
To sometimes split infinitives
To get words of out order
To punctuate,-badly
To confused my tenses
To deem old words wondrous fair
to ignore capitals
To employ common or garden clichés
To miss the occasional out
To indulge in tautological repetitive statements
To exaggerate hundreds of times a day
And to repeat puns quite by chants.
But worst of all I used
To forget to finish what I

A Siamese twin
Is someone with a strong
Family Thai

Is someone
Who needs no introduction
Beyond compère?

She's the kind of lasso
Will ring you
Quoit unexpectedly
And once she's round
You can't halter
Flow of noose

As a bank manager
My only interest
Is to get you a loan
And make advances

I feel so strongly
About loo graffiti
That I've signed
A partition

JOB ASSOCIATIONS

I remember
Sue veneers.
Chemists say
Anna lies.
Bulls know
Matt adores.
Sailors understand
Sam pans

Old age is when
Your heir apparent
Becomes a parent

After another woman
Had turned his head
He couldn't face his wife

If English printers
Sing in quires
Do French ones
Sing in reams?

Spanish Fly
Is strong stuff.
You only need
Half a Si Si

I dislike you some days
But love unites